THE
SEVERN
VALLEY
RAILWAY

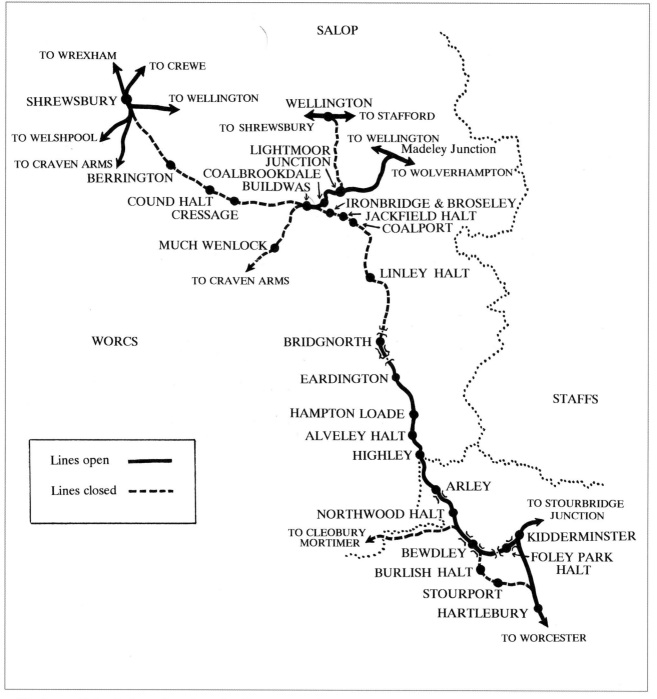

The Severn Valley Railway. (*Map drawn by Christine Siviter*)

THE
SEVERN
VALLEY
RAILWAY

ROGER SIVITER ARPS

SUTTON PUBLISHING

Sutton Publishing Limited
Phoenix Mill · Thrupp · Stroud
Gloucestershire · GL5 2BU

First published 2002

Copyright © Roger Siviter, 2002

British Library Cataloguing in Publication Data
A catalogue record for this book is available from the
British Library.

ISBN 0-7509-2976-6

Typeset in 10.5/13.5 Photina.
Typesetting and origination by
Sutton Publishing Limited.
Printed and bound in England by
J.H. Haynes & Co. Ltd, Sparkford.

Bewdley, 12 December 1981.

CONTENTS

Introduction   7

1.   Pre-Preservation Days   9

2.   Bridgnorth to Hampton Loade   31

3.   Hampton Loade to Bewdley   67

4.   Bewdley to Kidderminster   93

5.   SVR Locomotives on the Main Line   111

Bibliography   128

Colour Plates   129

LMS Stanier Class 5 4–6–0 No. 45110 *RAF Biggin Hill* is caught by the camera as it climbs the 1 in 100 up to Eardington station with an afternoon Highley to Bridgnorth train on 14 April 1974. No. 45110 was one of the locomotives used on the BR 'Farewell to Steam' special train on 11 August 1968, and after preservation at Ashford in January 1969 by the Stanier Black Five Preservation Society, it moved to the Severn Valley Railway (SVR) in August 1970. Originally unnamed, it was named on 12 September 1971 (see picture on page 68) and bought by the SVR in 1974. It has also been passed for running on BR and has been in charge of many main line special charter trains over recent years.

INTRODUCTION

The Severn Valley Railway (SVR) as we know it today runs some 16 miles from Bridgnorth, in the county of Shropshire, via Bewdley to its terminus at Kidderminster, crossing into Worcestershire just south of Arley, 7 miles from the famous carpet town.

The original Severn Valley route ran from Shrewsbury to Hartlebury (for Worcester) via Stourport plus the branch from Bewdley to Kidderminster on the Snow Hill, Stourbridge Junction and Worcester line. Although we deal with the history and the pre-preservation days in the first chapter, this book is primarily about the SVR as we know it today, from its beginnings in the 1960s right through to present times, and wherever possible using pictures that have not been seen before. I know with my own SVR pictures that a great many have never even been printed before!

In compiling this book I should like to thank the following people, without whose help it would not have been possible: Hugh Ballantyne, Roger Carpenter, John Dew, Barrie Geens, Michael Mensing, David Postle, Malcolm Ranieri FRPS, Godfrey Stewart, John Tennant, my wife Christina, my editor Simon Fletcher, and last but not least, all the volunteers and staff of the SVR who make it such a wonderful railway.

Roger Siviter
Evesham 2002

NOTE. Unless otherwise stated, all pictures were taken by Roger Siviter.

This early scene on the then newly preserved SVR could well be called 'Brief Encounter'. The date of this picture was 5 April 1969, one of the many open days that were held before the official re-opening of the line on 23 May 1970. The location is platform two at Bridgnorth station with LMS 8F 2–8–0 No. 48773 (later No. 8233) just visible by the goods shed.

1
Pre-Preservation Days

The original Severn Valley line from Shrewsbury to Hartlebury Junction was first authorised in 1853 and opened some nine years later on 1 February 1862. The first company to operate the line was the West Midland Railway, but on the 18 July 1872 the SVR was vested in the Great Western Railway.

The length of the line from Shrewsbury to Hartlebury was some 39½ miles plus the 3½ miles of the Bewdley to Kidderminster branch.

At Buildwas Junction, 11 miles south of Shrewsbury, and also equidistant between Shropshire's ancient county town and Bridgnorth, the line connected with the Wellington to Craven Arms branch, which formed a rail link between the LNWR west coast main line at Stafford (via Wellington) and Craven Arms on the GWR/LNWR joint line, situated on the Shrewsbury and Hereford line – the North to West route. This branch line was opened in the 1860s and closed in 1962. One mile north of Bewdley, just south of Northwood Halt, was the point where the line from Woofferton Junction (on the Shrewsbury to Hereford route) and Tenbury Wells converged with the SVR, both lines running side by side for around a mile to just before Bewdley station. This line opened in 1861 and closed completely in 1965.

Just south of Bewdley station is the junction for the short branch to Kidderminster, situated on the Stourbridge Junction to Worcester line. Today the SVR has its own splendid station at Kidderminster, which was built on the old goods yard. It also, very importantly, has a connection with the Stourbridge to Worcester line, just south of Kidderminster BR station.

The main SVR line ran south of Bewdley through the popular riverside resort of Stourport before meeting the Snow Hill to Stourbridge Junction to Worcester line at Hartlebury Junction. In BR days the main passenger traffic was in the hands of GWR and Standard 2–6–2 tank locomotives, and also GWR railcars and BR DMU sets.

Freight traffic was mostly coal trains from Highley to the power station at Stourport (which closed in 1980) and also to Ironbridge power station, next to Buildwas Junction. This power station, which is still open, was – and is today – serviced by MGR coal trains from Madeley junction on the Wolverhampton to Shrewsbury line which run via Coalbrookdale to Buildwas, this last section being the only part of the old Wellington to Craven Arms branch which remains today.

On 9 September 1963 passenger traffic ceased between Shrewsbury and Bewdley, and from Bewdley to Hartlebury and Kidderminster on 5 January 1970. By this latter date the remaining goods traffic (which was mainly coal trains) had finished with two exceptions, from Kidderminster to Foley Park sugar works, and Hartlebury to the CEGB power station at Stourport, both of which finished in 1980.

So now we turn our attention to the SVR as it is today from Bridgnorth to Bewdley and Kidderminster.

The man behind the idea of preserving part of the SVR line from Bridgnorth to Hampton Loade was Keith Beddoes from Kidderminster. The Severn Valley Railway Society was formed on 6 July 1965 at a meeting at the Cooper's Arms in Kidderminster. A few months later, on 3 February 1966, the Society made an offer to BR, which was accepted, of £2,500 for the land, buildings and track from Bridgnorth to just south of Hampton Loade station, subject to the granting of a light railway order by the Minister of Transport. Over the next few years, until the official re-opening of the line from Bridgnorth to Hampton Loade on 23 May 1970, a tremendous amount of work was done on the line and many successful open days were held, raising much-needed cash with which to purchase the line.

After the re-opening of the line in 1970 and with the support of Sir Gerald Nabbarro (formerly MP for Kidderminster and then Worcestershire South) the SVR were able to purchase the line down to Foley Park. This was completed in 1972, and after much civil engineering work, including considerable reconstruction of the Victoria Bridge, the service from Bridgnorth to Bewdley commenced on 18 May 1974 (the service from Bridgnorth to Highley having commenced a few weeks earlier on 12 April 1974).

With the end of rail traffic to the sugar factory at Foley Park in 1980 and the closure of Kidderminster goods yard in 1983 the SVR launched a successful share offer for the purchase of the remainder of the line to Kidderminster and the construction of a new terminus station on the goods yard site. The platform at the new station was completed on 24 May 1984, and trackwork laid. The light railway order was granted on 21 July 1984, and passenger trains commenced working on 30 July 1984. The first train, a VIP special, was headed by GWR Hall Class 4–6–0 No. 4930 *Hagley Hall*.

With the help of a grant from the English Tourist Board, work commenced on the station building in the autumn of 1984, and it was opened in September 1985.

The 25 March 1967 was an historic day for the 'new' SVR. It saw the arrival at Bridgnorth of its first locomotive, GWR Class '2251' 0–6–0 No. 3205, and some of the first rolling stock for the newly preserved line – four coaches. No. 3205 was restored at Buckfastleigh during 1965 and 1966 and then moved to Stourbridge by diesel in February 1967. It then ran on the Severn Valley Special on 25 March of that year from Stourbridge to Bridgnorth via Kidderminster.
Left: The special on its journey to Bridgnorth passing through Blakedown (on the Stourbridge to Worcester line) on that rather dull but epoch-making March day.
Below: The locomotive and stock after arrival at Bridgnorth station, the locomotive having run round its train and now facing Bewdley. (*Bottom picture: John Dew*)

The original Severn Valley Line started at the GWR/LMS joint station of Shrewsbury. In August 1963 a BR Standard Class 4 2–6–4 tank No. 80078 waits to leave bay platform No. 6 with a Severn Valley line train. Shrewsbury originally had an overall roof but this was removed in 1963. Note the ornate screen (also soon to be removed) on the right-hand side, which formed the side of the overhead roof. (*John Tennant*)

Leaving Shrewsbury, the SVR line leaves the Hereford and Cambrian lines at Sutton Bridge junction, some half a mile south of Shrewsbury station. On 28 May 1966 the down 'Cambrian Coast Express' hauled by BR Standard Class 4MT 4–6–0 No. 75006 approaches Sutton Bridge junction signal box. The SVR line can be seen swinging away behind the signal box. In a few yards the Cambrian line will diverge westwards from the Hereford line. In the background is Shrewsbury locomotive shed.

Although this picture at Sutton Bridge junction was taken as recently as 30 September 1989, the junction for the Severn Valley line (to the right of the train) can still be seen, although truncated a few feet further on. It has now been removed, together with the right-hand running line. The train in this view is the 1035 Shrewsbury to Cardiff service, hauled by Class 37 No. 37407 *Loch Long*, a pleasant reminder of when these popular English Electric Type 3 locomotives dominated the passenger workings in this area. Overlooking the scene is Shrewsbury Abbey, which dates from medieval times.

We are now on the SVR proper at Cressage, some 7½ miles south of Shrewsbury. This picture was taken on 29 August 1963, and shows ex-LMS Class 2MT 2–6–2 tank locomotive No. 41209 pulling into the station with a Shrewsbury-bound train. Note the splendid station house, which happily is now privately owned and which still retains the small platform canopy, seen to the left of the train. (*John Tennant*)

Buildwas Junction, midway between Shrewsbury and Bridgnorth, and where the Wellington to Much Wenlock and Craven Arms line intersected the Severn Valley route, is our next location. On 23 June 1962 ex-GWR Railcar No. W 20 pulls into the station with the 2.05 p.m. Kidderminster to Shrewsbury service. Out of the picture on the left-hand side is Ironbridge power station, which is built by the side of the River Severn. There is still a rail link from the power station, for MGR coal traffic, to Madeley junction on the Wolverhampton to Shrewsbury route, which runs via the old Wellington branch to Coalbrookdale and Lightmoor junction, and then to Madeley junction. (*John Tennant*)

After leaving Buildwas, the line follows the River Severn more or less all the way to Bewdley, running through Ironbridge (home of the Industrial Revolution) and passing through Coalport, where on 12 July 1962 an ex-GWR Class 41XX 2–6–2 prairie tank locomotive is seen heading through Coalport (GWR) station with a northbound coal train. Like many of the station houses on the SVR between Shrewsbury and Bridgnorth, this is now in private hands. On the eastern side of the river was the LNWR Coalport station, terminus of the branch from Oakengates and Wellington (for Stafford). The whole of this area around Ironbridge, Jackfield and Coalport has now become famous as a heritage site throughout the world as the birthplace of the Industrial Revolution. (*John Tennant*)

Bridgnorth station was opened in 1862, as were all the main stations on the line. Just over 100 years later, on 6 September 1963, ex-LMS Class 2MT 2–6–2 tank No. 41209 stands at platform one of Bridgnorth station waiting to leave on the 7.27 p.m. train to Shrewsbury. On 9 September, within a few days of this picture being taken, passenger services between Shrewsbury and Bewdley would cease – one of the many casualties of the Beeching cuts. (*Hugh Ballantyne*)

This second view of Bridgnorth station (looking north) was taken in about 1960 and shows the fine-looking station building and surrounding infrastructure to full advantage. Note the GWR billboards on the right-hand side and also the hanging flower baskets. (*Joe Moss*)

Our next location in BR days is Hampton Loade, some 4½ miles from Bridgnorth and 26 miles from Shropshire's county town, Shrewsbury. This picture of Hampton Loade station, looking north, was taken in 1962, a year before the cessation of passenger services. It is interesting to make a comparison with this scene and the station as it is today (see pictures on pages 68 and 69) (*Roger Siviter Collection*)

Arguably the most industrial location on the Severn Valley line was Highley, which boasted several collieries. Alveley colliery was situated just north of Highley station but on the other side of the River Severn, with a connection to the rail head at Alveley colliery sidings by means of an aerial ropeway over a concrete river bridge. There was also a halt near the sidings for the mineworkers. To the west of Highley station (connected by a rail link) was situated Highley colliery. This colliery was closed for winding coal in 1939, and Alveley in 1969.

This view of Highley station, looking north, was taken in 1958. In the foreground is the now dismantled cattle loading dock, and beyond that the lengthy footbridge which led to the road to the town, which was roughly a mile from the station. This footbridge was demolished in 1974. It is also worth pointing out that Highley is also a large farming area, and these days it is a busy tourist area. (*Joe Moss*)

Just over 2 miles south of Highley and still on the western side of the river is Arley station. This view, looking north, was taken in about 1958 and shows the station to be in almost pristine condition. However, after the station's closure by BR in 1963 the signals and the up (right-hand side) line were removed and the station was soon looking very run down. Restoration work by the SVR began in 1972 and the station re-opened in 1974 in readiness for the new passenger service between Bewdley and Bridgnorth. (*Joe Moss*)

Another picture of 8F 2–8–0 No. 48460 taken on 7 July 1966, this time a couple of hours earlier than the previous two scenes. No. 48460 is seen near Northwood heading for Highley and Alveley colliery with empty coal wagons from Stourport power station. This picture gives some idea of the state of the trackwork and surrounding vegetation prior to complete closure by BR of this section of the line on 3 February 1969.

Opposite: Shortly after leaving Arley the line crosses the River Severn by means of the Victoria Bridge, and is also now in the county of Worcestershire. These two pictures, taken on 7 July 1966 between Arley and Northwood, show ex-LMS Class 8F 2–8–0 No. 48460 with a Highley to Stourport power station coal train as it skirts the eastern side of the river. The second view shows how close the line is to the river bank, and also shows the aqueduct bridge which connects with Trimpley reservoirs on the eastern side of the line.

A busy scene at Bewdley station on the evening of 6 September 1963. On the far left a three-car DMU set is waiting to leave for Kidderminster. In the centre a Gloucester Railway Carriage & Wagon Co. single diesel unit No. W 55005 waits to leave with the 4.20 p.m. Shrewsbury to Hartlebury, while sister unit No. W 55004 is about to leave platform one with the 6.24 p.m. Hartlebury to Bridgnorth. Passenger services between Shrewsbury and Bewdley ended on 9 September 1963 but the passenger services from Bewdley to Hartlebury and Kidderminster carried on until 5 January 1970. It is nice to know that with the preservation of the line between Bridgnorth and Kidderminster, Bewdley station is still a hive of activity. (*Hugh Ballantyne*)

Opposite, top: After Northwood was the junction, or divergence, for Tenbury Wells. On 20 June 1959 BR Standard Class 3 2–6–2 tank No. 82004 passes the Tenbury line as it heads for Bewdley with the 1.45 p.m. Shrewsbury to Hartlebury train. These two lines ran side by side to Bewdley where, just north of the station, trains from Tenbury gained access to the Kidderminster line by crossover points, and of course vice versa. (*Michael Mensing*)

Opposite, bottom: There are six viaducts between Kidderminster and Bridgnorth including Wribbenhall (or Bewdley) viaduct, a few yards north of Bewdley station. On 29 June 1966 8F 2–8–0 No. 48531 propels a brake van over the 112 yard-long viaduct and heads for the colliery sidings at Highley.

The coal trains from Highley to Stourport ran until 3 February 1969 and were hauled by steam locomotives, latterly mainly 8F 2–8–0s off Stourbridge shed (2C), until the closure of the shed to steam in July 1966, when diesel traction took over these duties. On 30 June 1966 ex-LMS 8F 2–8–0 No. 48531 pulls through the smart-looking station at Bewdley with a load of coal for Stourport power station.

Just south of Bewdley station, before the junction of the Kidderminster and Hartlebury lines is another viaduct – Sandbourne – which has 10 arches and is 101 yards long. On 23 May 1966 8F 2–8–0 No. 48459 propels its brake van over the viaduct and heads for Bewdley and Highley for another load of power station coal.

Although at this point the line appears to be double track it is in fact two single lines, the nearer one being to Stourport. No. 48459 is coming into Bewdley on the line from Kidderminster, so it has probably come straight from Stourbridge shed (2C).

We are now on the Stourport to Hartlebury section of the Severn Valley route at Burlish Halt, situated just to the north-west of Stourport. This view of Burlish Halt, taken in 1962 looking to Stourport, shows the typical GWR-style 'pagoda' waiting room or shelter; note also the ornate lighting. The halt was opened in 1930 and closed in 1970 with the termination of passenger services between Bewdley and Hartlebury. Today this whole area is a large housing estate, with only the crossing keeper's cottage (just half a mile north-west of the halt, at the site of Burlish crossing) as a reminder of past days. (*Roger Siviter Collection*)

Our next location is Stourport-on-Severn, a principal station on the route with not only a branch line to Stourport power station to the south of the station but also, to the north of the station, sidings and a line running to the canal basin of the Staffordshire & Worcestershire Canal. The last BR coal train from Hartlebury ran to the power station in March 1979, and canal traffic ceased in the early 1960s. Stourport, like Bewdley, was and still is a popular day out with people from Birmingham and the Black Country, and during BR days many excursions were run to the riverside resorts. This view of Stourport station, looking towards Bewdley, was taken in about 1958 and shows the level crossing gates which controlled the line over the A451 road from Kidderminster. Today the station site is a housing estate. (*Joe Moss*)

Two miles from Stourport the Severn Valley line joined the Worcester to Stourbridge line at Hartlebury junction, just under a mile north of Hartlebury station. This photograph, taken in August 1963, shows the impressive station nameboard at Hartlebury station. All traffic between Stourport and Hartlebury ceased on 1 October 1980, the last coal train having been worked in March 1979. (*P.J. Garland Collection*)

We are now on the Bewdley to Kidderminster section of the line, sometimes known as the Kidderminster loop line. This picture, taken at Birchen Coppice around 1 mile from Bewdley and 2 miles from Kidderminster, shows 8F 2–8–0 No. 48460 heading for Kidderminster and the Birmingham area with coal from Alveley colliery on 5 July 1966. With the finish of rail traffic to Foley Park sugar beet works in 1980, and the closure of Kidderminster goods yard in 1983, the SVR was able to complete its extension into Kidderminster, and the service from Bewdley to the carpet town started on 30 July 1984, a platform having been built in the goods yard with a run-round loop. By 28 September of the following year the new station had been completed and opened to the public.

In the summer of 1953 ex-GWR Class 4300 2–6–0 No. 6306 poses by the coaling ramp of Kidderminster locomotive shed (85D). This shed was situated on the south side of the SVR line, just before the junction with the Stourbridge to Worcester line. It opened in 1932 with two locomotive roads, accommodating up to sixteen engines in its heyday, including the Cleobury Mortimer & Ditton Priors Light Railway pannier tanks Nos 28 and 29. This famous light railway ran for 11 miles north-west from Cleobury Mortimer (on the Tenbury line) to its terminus at Ditton Priors. The line closed completely in 1965. (*Roger Carpenter Collection*)

Ex-GWR Hall Class 4–6–0 No. 5983 *Henley Hall* leaves Kidderminster for Worcester with an up stopping train, *c*. 1960. This picture shows part of the goods yard which was to become the site of the new SVR station complex. Out of sight behind the photographer is the junction for the Severn Valley line. (*P.C. Wheeler*)

We are now at Kidderminster station, situated on the Stourbridge to Worcester line where, on 3 July 1961, ex-GWR railcar No. W 24 arrives at the platform to form the 2.05 p.m. to Bridgnorth and Shrewsbury. This station had an Elizabethan-style frontage, but was replaced by a more functional design later in that decade. (*John Dew*)

2

Bridgnorth to Hampton Loade

Although the SVR Preservation Society was formed on 6 July 1965, and the section from Bridgnorth to just south of Hampton Loade was bought in 1966, it was another four years, on 23 May 1970, before the official re-opening of the line, with trains running from Bridgnorth to Hampton Loade. However, in that four-year period open days were held at Bridgnorth station, and with the arrival on 25 March 1967 of GWR 0–6–0 No. 3205 and four coaches, and LMS 2–6–0 No. 46443 on 22 April 1967, these open events were extended to two and three days, attracting many hundreds of visitors who took out day membership tickets, enabling them to travel on the shuttle service to Oldbury viaduct and back. Then in April 1968, after much work on the trackside, members-only trips were run to Hampton Loade and return.

On 15 April 1968 No. 3205 waits to leave Bridgnorth station with a Hampton Loade train. This was the first weekend of the 'extended' shuttle trains. Note the dozens of people on the platform and signs of track maintenance work on the right-hand side. ´

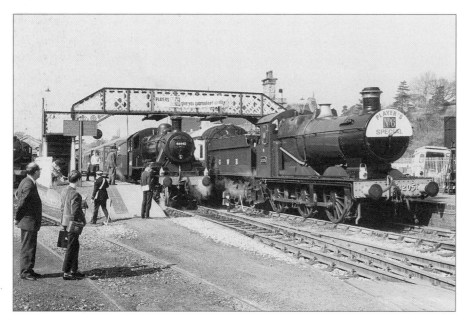

This picture was taken a year later on 5 April 1969 and this time shows No. 46443 waiting to leave on a Hampton Loade train, with No. 3205 on a promotional train for John Player cigarettes. On the left-hand edge of the picture can just be seen LMS Class 4MT 2–6–0 No. 43106 in the shed yard. No. 43106 was one of the last of its class to work on BR, being withdrawn from Lostock Hall depot, Preston, on 23 June 1968. It was then bought by eighteen SVR members and ran in steam to Bridgnorth in August 1968.

To complete this trio of open day pictures, we see No. 3205 once again as it prepares to leave Bridgnorth on 1 September 1968 with a Hampton Loade train. This picture well illustrates the crowds that turned up for these early open days, all eager to see and ride behind steam locomotives once again.

No. 3205 at Bridgnorth, 5 April 1969.

Opposite, top: A similar scene to the previous picture but this time taken some thirty-three years later on 12 October 2001. On the left is ex-LMS 8F 2–8–0 No. 48773 with the 1.30 p.m. to Kidderminster, with ex-LNER A4 Pacific No. 60009 *Union of South Africa* looking on. In the distance is an English Electric Class 37 diesel and behind it a 'Western' Class hydraulic diesel. Comparison with the previous picture will show many similarities, and some differences – the major being the extension of number one platform.

Opposite, bottom: This picture was taken on 15 August 1994 and shows GWR Class 28XX 2–8–0 No. 2857 pulling into platform one of Bridgnorth station with the 3.30 p.m. train from Kidderminster. These fine-looking locomotives were designed by Churchward and introduced in 1903, No. 2857 being built in 1918. Although primarily goods locomotives, on busy summer Saturdays they were often found on passenger trains to the West Country – notably the 1.30 p.m. Paddington to Kingswear.

SVR locomotive superintendent Arthur Becker takes a hard look at ex-LMS 2MT No. 46443 and also ex-LMS Black Five 4–6–0 No. 45110 as they stand in Bridgnorth station on Thursday 2 March 1972. The locomotives were in steam for a special filming by the BBC. Over the years many films have been made by TV and film companies using the SVR notably, in more recent times, *Oh, Dr Beeching!*, a comedy series made by the BBC and set in and around Arley station, starring Sue Pollard and Paul Shane. In 1976 Universal Films made *The Seven Per Cent Solution*, starring Nicol Williamson and Vanessa Redgrave. This is a Sherlock Holmes film, set in and around Vienna, with the European railway scenes being staged on the SVR, mainly featuring 2–6–0 No. 46443 (in red livery with the first two numbers blotted out) and 5MT 4–6–0 No. 45110, with also the odd glimpse of LMS 8F 2–8–0 No. 8233 and GWR 45XX 2–6–2 tank No. 4566.

No. 46443 receives attention in Bridgnorth
shed yard on 21 October 1972.

On a very cold New Year's Eve 1973 0–6–0 saddle tank No. 193 takes water at Bridgnorth station before leaving with the 12.30 to Hampton Loade. This locomotive was built by Hunslet of Leeds (works No. 3793) in 1953 to a War Department design and then bought by the Army, working mainly on the Shropshire & Montgomeryshire Light Railway between Shrewsbury and Llanymynech. On 20 March 1960 it worked the last train on the S&MLR, this being organised by the Stephenson Locomotive Society. It then spent most of the next eleven years in storage at Long Marston camp near Stratford-upon-Avon, moving to the SVR at Bridgnorth by road on 7 August 1971. Originally in a dark green livery, it was repainted in crimson lake and named *Shropshire* in 1977. Also note, in the background, GWR diesel railcar No. 22.

A true winter's day at Bridgnorth on Sunday 27 December 1970. In the station is GWR diesel railcar No. 22. This railcar was one of a batch built in 1940. It had seating for forty-eight people, and worked regularly on the line in BR days. This view, looking north towards Bridgnorth tunnel, shows not only the goods shed but the station signal box. This box is not the original. After the line was partially closed in 1963 Bridgnorth box was dismantled but the base was retained. In 1968–9 the upper part of the box was replaced by the superstructure from Pensnett (near Brierley Hill) signal box, the base being modified to fit the new shorter signal box.

Still with a wintry feel, 0–6–0 saddle tank, No. 193 departs with the 12.30 p.m. to Hampton Loade on 31 December 1973.

Another War Department locomotive at work on the Severn Valley is 2–10–0 No. 600 *Gordon* (named after General Gordon). It was built in 1943 by the North British Locomotive Company at Glasgow, and spent all its life at the Army railway depot at Longmoor in Hampshire, being used for instruction purposes. It moved to the SVR in the early 1970s. This close-up of the powerful 2–10–0 leaving Bridgnorth with the 4 p.m. to Hampton Loade train was taken on 30 June 1973. Note also the Gilt-Edge carpets exhibition coach on the right-hand side.

This view illustrates the shed area at Bridgnorth in its early days. The picture, taken on 24 May 1970, shows LMS 8F 2–8–0 No. 8233 (later No. 48773) in the shed area which then used the old goods shed (just out of sight) and the surrounding huts and sidings. At the side of the 8F can just be seen 0–6–0 ST No. 2047 *Warwickshire*.

Still in the old shed area, as ex-LMS Class 4 MT No. 43106 is coaled, in July 1974. The old goods shed can be seen clearly at the rear of the locomotives.

This view, taken on 23 August 1980, shows the splendid new three road shed and workshop, which opened in 1978. Clearly visible are GWR Manor Class 4–6–0 No. 7819 *Hinton Manor*, WD 2–10–0 No. 600 *Gordon* and once again No. 43106.

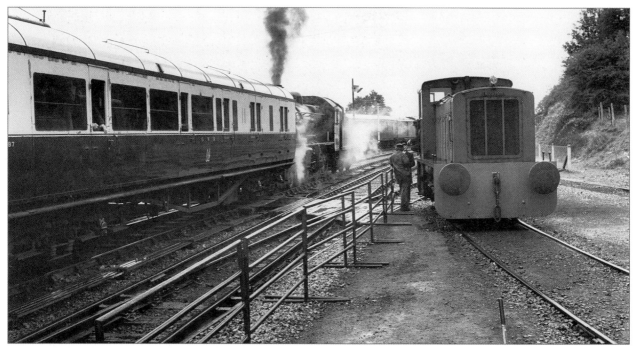

Nearly every preserved line has a small diesel locomotive, used for shunting, etc. This is often known as the yard, or shed, 'goat'. On 13 August 1974 0–4–0 diesel No. 319290 pauses at the entrance to the shed area, while 2–6–0 No. 46443 prepares to leave with a train for Bewdley. This 165 hp diesel locomotive was built by Ruston Hornsby at their Lincoln works in 1953, and after many years of industrial work at Ellesmere Port and then Oldbury now finds useful employment on the SVR, where it arrived in 1972. Note also the beautifully restored GWR coach, one of many in use on the line.

View from the train. GWR Class 57XX 0–6–0 pannier tank No. 5764 is seen in the shed yard on 30 June 1973. No. 5764 was built at Swindon in 1929 by the Great Western Railway and operated mainly in the London area. In 1960 it was sold by BR to London Transport and numbered L95. The SVR bought the locomotive in 1971 and used it for a season in the London Transport livery (see picture on page 61) before restoration to the GW livery in 1972.

The SVR at Bridgnorth has always been famous for overhauling locomotives, and also getting them back into (BR) main line condition. Two such locomotives that have seen much main line working over recent years have been ex-LMS Class 6P5F 2–6–0 No. 42968 and BR Standard Class 4 MT 4–6–0 No. 75069, seen here in the shed yard at Bridgnorth on 13 August 1974, prior to restoration work. No. 75069 came to the SVR at Bewdley from the famous Barry scrapyard on 31 March 1973, and No. 42968 came from Barry to Bewdley on 14 December 1973. Both locomotives were then hauled to Bridgnorth by No. 46443 in July 1974.

A busy scene at Bridgnorth as 0–6–0 saddle tank No. 193 approaches the station with a train from Hampton Loade and 2–6–0 No. 43106 waits to leave with a Bewdley train, 7 July 1974.

For the first mile out of Bridgnorth trains to Hampton Loade face a steep climb at around 1 in 100. On Open Day 2 September 1968 LMS 2–6–0 No. 43106 darkens the sky as it heads south out of Bridgnorth with a Hampton Loade train.

On 24 July 1975 GWR Class 45XX 'small prairie' 2–6–2 tank No. 4566 pulls out of Bridgnorth station with the 2.15 p.m. to Bewdley. This picture was taken a few days after the locomotive had been restored and returned to traffic. It came from Barry scrapyard in August 1970 after being there since the summer of 1962. In the background of the picture, across the valley, can be seen Castle Hill, access to which at the time could be gained by a lengthy footbridge from the station. This footbridge was closed in 1976, but thanks to the efforts of the Bridgnorth Footbridge Trust a new footbridge was erected and opened in 1994.

No. 3205 heads out of Bridgnorth on 2 September 1968 with an afternoon train to Hampton Loade.

A few yards from the previous pictures, the line crosses over the B4363 to Cleobury Mortimer. On 2 March 1972 ex-LMS 2–6–0 No. 46443 is seen running down into the station in order to take out a train for Hampton Loade, all this to be filmed by the BBC (see picture on pages 36 and 37). Today the road has been straightened out and also slightly raised, and new lighting installed. The cars are now also of interest; on the left-hand side is an Austin 1100 and on the right is a Riley 1300, both manufactured by British Leyland.

On 1 January 1980 GWR Class 51XX 2–6–2 tank No. 5164 crosses the Cleobury Mortimer road and heads south with a Bridgnorth to Hampton Loade train. Note the fine GWR bracket signal.

On New Year's Day 1980 GWR Class 51XX No. 5164 with a Hampton Loade train runs through the wooded section of the line at Oldbury, just south of Bridgnorth. No. 5164 had just entered service after many years of careful restoration work, and looks a credit to all who worked on her.

Opposite, top: A few yards further on from the previous picture is 0–6–0 No. 193 as it heads for Hampton Loade on 23 December 1973 with the 2.30 p.m. train from Bridgnorth, a 'Father Christmas special'. This view gives some idea of how Bridgnorth town was expanding around this time, with many new houses being built to accommodate its growing population.

Opposite, bottom: On 21 November 1981 LMS Jubilee Class 4–6–0 No. 5690 *Leander* heads out of Bridgnorth with a special train to Hampton Loade. Extensive boiler repairs had just been completed on the locomotive, and at a ceremony that day at Bridgnorth station the Commander of HMS *Leander*, H.S. Drake, relaunched the locomotive by unveiling 5690's nameplate. This was followed by the special run to mark the occasion. This location is a few yards south of the new bypass railway bridge, the bypass having opened on 29 March 1985, some fifteen years after negotiations between the SVR and Shropshire County Council, which culminated in a sharing of costs (30 per cent by the SVR and the rest by the County Council) for the construction of the bridge. At one time it was feared that, because of the bypass, Bridgnorth station site would have to be abandoned and another station built to the south of the bypass, but the construction of the bridge thankfully saved the station.

Heading south down the line our next location is the five-arch Oldbury viaduct where on 8 October 1994 English Electric Class 50 No. 50044 *Exeter* heads north for Bridgnorth with an engineers' special train. Notice that the viaduct (which at this point crosses over Daniel's Mill) was originally built for double track.

A few hundred yards south of Oldbury viaduct is the short tunnel at Knowlesands, also of double track width. On 27 May 1973 LMS 8F No. 8233 (now 48773) is seen just north of the tunnel with the 2 p.m. Bridgnorth to Hampton Loade train.

At the same location as the previous picture, only taken from the other side of the track, we see GWR railcar No. 22 on one of its rare outings, a return shoppers' special from Bridgnorth to Hampton Loade on the afternoon of Saturday 13 October 1974.

This view is taken from just inside Knowlesands tunnel and shows GWR 0–6–0 No. 3205 as it approaches the tunnel with a Bridgnorth to Hampton Loade train on 24 May 1970. In this picture we can clearly see that the tunnel was built for possible double track use.

No. 3205 once again, this time coasting down Eardington bank (south of Knowlesands) with the 5.10 p.m. Bridgnorth to Hampton Loade train, 30 June 1973.

To complete this trio of pictures of No. 3205, we see this popular GWR locomotive at the head of an 'open day' special train to Hampton Loade on 15 April 1968. The location is the top of Eardington bank.

This side view of 2–10–0 *Gordon* climbing Eardington bank on 14 April 1974 with a Hampton Loade for Bridgnorth train gives some idea of the size of this powerful locomotive, which has a tractive effort of 34,215 lbs.

Opposite, top: Another side view of Eardington bank, this time LMS 8F 2–8–0 No. 8233 with a Bridgnorth train on 27 May 1973. This locomotive was built by the North British Locomotive Company at Glasgow in 1940, and after a short spell on the LMS it worked for the War Department in the Middle East from 1941 to 1952, when it returned to Derby for overhaul, and then moved to the Longmoor Military Railway. In 1959 No. 8233 was purchased by BR, where it worked until it was preserved in 1968 by the Stanier 8F Locomotive Society, and arrived on the SVR on 4 January 1969. Also note the train of LMS stock with, next to the engine, an LMS Stanier passenger brake van, built at Wolverton LMS carriage and wagon works in 1932. These six-wheel vehicles are commonly called 'Stove Rs'.

Opposite, bottom: On 23 December 1973 WD 0–6–0 saddle tank No. 193 climbs the 1 in 100 of Eardington bank with an afternoon Hampton Loade to Bridgnorth train. Note the carriage stock, a mixture of LMS and GWR, a common sight in the early days of the SVR. Today the company has complete sets of stock, making the line even more authentic.

We saw pannier tank No. 5764 in an earlier picture (page 47) and this view of the pannier tank taken at Eardington station on 27 July 1971 taking water (with a train to Hampton Loade) shows it in its original London Transport livery, having arrived on the SVR a few weeks earlier, on 19 June.

Opposite: The first station south of Bridgnorth was Eardington Halt, roughly equidistant between there and Hampton Loade. Originally built to serve the local community, in the early days of the preserved line it was much used as an intermediate shopping place with watering facilities. However, after the line was fully opened to Bewdley in 1974 it was used less and less, and finally closed in 1982. On 31 March 1972 fireman Tony Bending 'waters' 2–6–0 No. 46443 as driver Gerry Carter looks on. The train is the 2 p.m. from Bridgnorth to Hampton Loade.

From Eardington to Bewdley the line more or less parallels the River Severn, crossing over it just south of Arley by means of the Victoria Bridge. About half a mile south of Eardington station is Hay Bridge where, on 30 September 1973, LNER Class K4 2–6–0 No. 3442 is caught by the camera as it climbs the 1 in 100 towards Eardington station and Bridgnorth with a train from Hampton Loade. This fine-looking 2–6–0 was one of six built by the LNER in 1937 to a design by Sir Nigel Gresley for use on the West Highland line, No. 3442 being named *The Great Marquess*. In 1962 it was bought from BR by Viscount Garnock (later to be President of the SVR) and was brought to the SVR in 1972, where for many years it was the sole representative of the LNER on the line, to be joined by Class A4 Pacific No. 60009 *Union of South Africa* in about 1990.

No. 3442 returned to main line duty in July 1989 with a spell of working on its original home territory, the Fort William to Mallaig line, known as the West Highland extension line (see pictures on page 122).

Another picture of Hay Bridge, this time of SVR stalwart ex-LMS 'Black Five' 4–6–0 No. 45110 as it climbs towards Eardington on 14 April 1974 with a Highley to Bridgnorth train, the service to Highley having commenced two days before on 12 April, to be followed on 18 May with trains through to Bewdley.

I mentioned earlier that No. 45110 was famous for having worked the first leg of the BR Last Steam Train ('15 Guinea Special') from Liverpool Lime Street to Manchester Victoria station on 11 August 1968. So I hope the reader will understand why I have included a picture that I took on that historical day of No. 45110 as it pulled into Rainhill station, to be greeted by hundreds of people. Rainhill was, of course, the site of the famous railway trials held in 1829–30.

The most powerful steam locomotive on the SVR (not including visiting engines) is ex-LNER A4 Pacific No. 60009 *Union of South Africa*, seen here at Sterns, just south of Hay Bridge, with the 11.30 a.m. Kidderminster to Bridgnorth train on 18 February 1990, shortly after a complete overhaul at Bridgnorth workshops.

A complete contrast to No. 60009, both in size and power, is 0–6–0 saddle tank No. 193, seen here on 1 April 1973 in the wooded section between Sterns and Hampton Loade with the 1.35 p.m. train from Hampton Loade to Bridgnorth. Mind you, with a tractive effort of 23,870 lbs it is still a very powerful locomotive for its size, and in the early days of the SVR it was in regular use on passenger workings.

Opposite, top: The ubiquitous No. 193 once again, this time pulling out of Hampton Loade (with the last train of the day) on the 4½ mile journey to Bridgnorth, on 31 December 1973.

Opposite, bottom: In late August 1967 GWR 0–6–0 No. 3205 arrives at Hampton Loade with a works train. Much work was done on the trackwork that following autumn and winter, prior to the open day shuttle services between Bridgnorth and Hampton Loade, which commenced in April the following year (1968). The splendid contemporary cars are now all of interest. They include an early Ford Cortina, soft-top Morris Minor, Hillman Imp and, right at the back, an early Austin Mini – probably all collector's items now. (*John Dew*)

This view of Hampton Loade station was taken with a telephoto lens on 2 May 1971, and shows the rear of 4–6–0 No. 45110 running round its train for the return journey to Bridgnorth.

3

Hampton Loade to Bewdley

This view of Hampton Loade station, looking to Bewdley, was taken on 21 October 2001, and a comparison with the picture in BR days (page 18) shows what has been achieved over the years of preservation by the volunteer station staff. I can also recommend the refreshment kiosk with its excellent tea and cakes, and also the railwayana to be seen in the waiting room. Note also the fine signal box which was more or less rebuilt from scratch. The station itself is only a few yards from the ferry crossing which connects Hampton, where the station is located, with Hampton Loade on the east side of the river.

An historic occasion at Hampton Loade station, on 12 September 1971, when ex-LMS Class 5 4–6–0 No. 45110 was named *RAF Biggin Hill*. Here the guard of honour, formed by a local unit of Air Training Corps cadets, is inspected by RAF officers Air Commodore Allan, Group Captain Rees, Squadron Leader Hearn and Squadron Leader Bayton-Hughes. (*John Dew*)

These two pictures at Hampton Loade once again provide quite a contrast. The scene above shows ex-GWR diesel railcar No. 22 in the stages of repainting to GWR chocolate-and-cream, about to leave the station and head for Bridgnorth in September 1968. The picture below, taken on 21 October 2001, shows BR Standard Class 4 MT 2–6–4 tank No. 80079 waiting to leave the station with the 10.30 a.m. Kidderminster to Bridgnorth service. Approaching the station is SR West Country Pacific No. 34027 *Taw Valley* with the 11.00 a.m. Bridgnorth to Kidderminster train. Hampton Loade is a standard crossing point for the regular service trains.

Another early scene at Hampton Loade on the open day of 13 April 1968, as No. 3205 pauses at the station with a train from Bridgnorth. The 0–6–0 will shortly run around its train for the return journey.

The 2 miles or so between Hampton Loade station and Highley were officially opened to passenger traffic on 12 April 1974. Halfway along this section of the SVR was situated Alveley Colliery Halt, which connected by a footbridge with the colliery which was located on the other side of the river. Above this bridge, which was situated to the south of the halt, was an aerial ropeway to convey the coal from the colliery to the nearby coal sidings. The colliery was closed in 1969 and the sidings dismantled, but the footbridge is still in place, now leading walkers to a country park. Also now on the site of the sidings is a new halt – Country Park Halt – which was built in 1996, and paid for by Bridgnorth District Council, to serve the Severn Valley Country Park. This picture, taken on 18 September 1994, shows the site of Alveley Colliery Halt. The train heading for Bridgnorth is the 1.30 p.m. from Kidderminster, with Class 25 diesel No. 7633 in charge.

Soon after leaving Highley station, northbound trains face a short climb of 1 in 100. On a wet 13 August 1974 ex-LMS Class 2 MT 2–6–0 No. 46443 darkens the sky as it pulls out of Highley with a Bridgnorth train.

When the line from Highley to Bewdley was officially opened on 18 May 1974, Arley station, after much restoration work, was opened in time for the new service, thus offering the traveller on the SVR another delightful country venue, with not only a ferry across the river to Upper Arley but also many riverside picnic and play areas within easy walking distance of the station. As can be seen in this picture, taken on 25 May 1975 (a year after the official opening), preservation work was still taking place. The SVR dismantled the original signal box shortly after the line was preserved, thinking that it would not be needed. However, it was soon obvious that a box was needed, so a signal box (ex-LNWR) from Yorton on the Shrewsbury to Crewe line was obtained and re-erected at Arley station. Approaching the station on that spring day is 2–6–0 No. 43106 with a Bridgnorth to Bewdley train.

Opposite, top: On the third day of the new service from Bridgnorth to Highley (14 April 1974) ex-WD 2–10–0 *Gordon* arrives at Highley station with a train from Bridgnorth. The footbridge seen in the picture on page 19 had just been demolished, with only one of the bases (seen just behind the people) then remaining. This station only ever had one platform, plus a passing loop and sidings, which still remain. Note also the original GWR signal box.

Opposite, bottom: Some twenty-seven years later, on 21 October 2001, ex-LMS Class 8F 2–8–0 No. 48773 (formerly LMS No. 8233) approaches Highley station from the south with the 11.45 a.m. Kidderminster to Bridgnorth service, and is about to pass the former LNWR water tank (from Whitchurch in Shropshire), which was erected in 1981. This is very convenient as Highley is roughly halfway between the line's termini. To take this picture I was standing on the restored cattle dock, a reminder that Highley was not only an industrial town but was (and still is) a busy farming area. Note also the spur line, now truncated, which led to Highley colliery. With its country parks adjacent to the station and the historic mining village (or town) with its twelfth-century Norman church, Highley is well worth a visit.

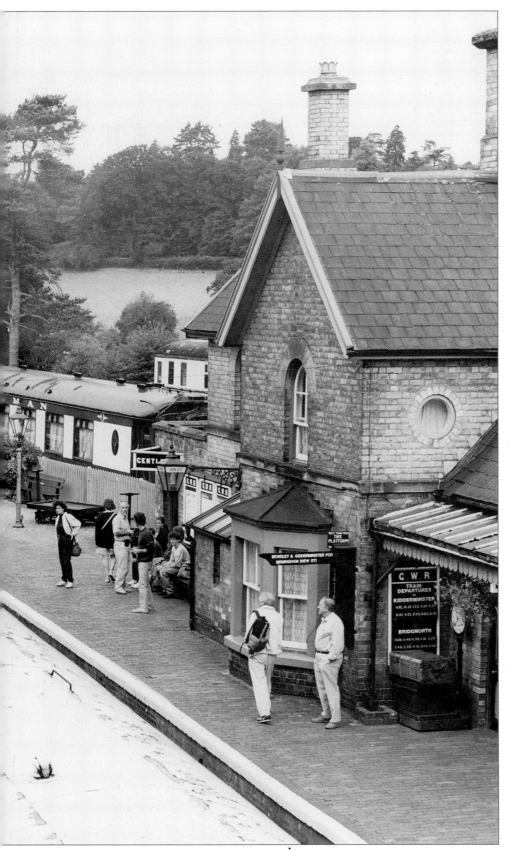

On 14 August 1994 GWR 2–6–0 No. 7325 enters Arley station with the 11.15 a.m. Kidderminster to Bridgnorth service. In the sidings next to the signal box are volunteers'/workmen's coaches and, stabled next to these, LMS Jubilee Class 4–6–0 No. 5690 *Leander*. Note the beautifully restored station buildings, a credit to the SVR volunteers who work on them.

GWR Manor Class 4–6–0 No. 7812 *Earlstoke Manor* pauses at Arley station on 20 June 1982 with a Bridgnorth to Bewdley train. Just visible in the siding beyond the station building is another Manor Class locomotive, probably No. 7819 *Hinton Manor*. The SVR has three of these fine-looking 4–6–0s on its books, the other engine being No. 7802 *Bradley Manor*. All these three locomotives came from Barry scrapyard at one time and another, and have been beautifully restored to main line running condition.

The SVR has a fine fleet of ex-BR diesel locomotives, including three of the popular 'Western' Class diesel hydraulic locomotives, built at the old GWR works at Swindon in the early 1960s. No. D 1062 *Western Courier* sets off from Arley on 14 August 1994 with the 12.35 p.m. Bridgnorth to Kidderminster service.

From the Bewdley direction Arley is approached through a steep cutting. On 20 June 1982 GWR 0–6–0 pannier tank No. 5764 threads that cutting with a fine-looking freight train made up of wagons, vans, a tanker and a brake van. Overlooking the scene is a GWR bracket signal.

The freight train hauled by No. 5764 is seen again, this time earlier in the day, crossing the Victoria Bridge and heading for Arley. The fishermen complete this quintessentially Severn Valley scene.

The single-span Victoria Bridge, which crosses the River Severn just south of Arley, is of cast-iron construction and was completed in 1861. On 28 September 1985 GWR City Class 4–4–0 No. 3440 *City of Truro* crosses the famous bridge with the 3.40 p.m. train from Bridgnorth to Kidderminster. No. 3440 had just been overhauled and restored to main line running condition at Bridgnorth workshops.

Another vintage engine crossing the Victoria Bridge, this time on the evening of 20 September 1986, is former LNWR Webb 'Coal Tank' No. 1054. These 0–6–2 tank engines were introduced in 1882. Over the years many locomotives have visited the line, including No. 1054, which at the time was shedded at Dinting Railway Centre. No. 3440 came from Swindon Railway Museum.

After being restored at Bridgnorth ex-LNER Class A4 4–6–2 No. 60009 *Union of South Africa* ran on the SVR before its trial trip on BR metals (see picture on page 121). The Pacific is seen heading off the Victoria Bridge with the 2.30 p.m. train from Kidderminster to Bridgnorth, 18 February 1990.

After leaving the Victoria Bridge the line to Bewdley then skirts the edge of Eymoor Wood. On 20 June 1982 GWR
Hall Class 4–6–0 No. 4930 *Hagley Hall* is seen in this heavily wooded section with a Bridgnorth to Bewdley train.
Hagley Hall was built at Swindon in 1929, and on withdrawal in November 1963 it was sold to Woodham Bros at
Barry for cutting up, where it arrived in April 1964. After eight years in the scrapyard awaiting its fate it was bought
by the SVR, and arrived at Bewdley in January 1973. After much renovation it returned to service in 1979, both on
the SVR and on main line duties. *Hagley Hall* has close connections with the SVR, being the name of the
Worcestershire ancestral home of the late President of the SVR Company, Viscount Cobham.

A complete contrast to the previous scene, as GWR 0–6–0 pannier tank No. 5764 heads through the woods between Northwood Halt and Victoria Bridge with a Bewdley to Bridgnorth train on a very wintry 18 March 1977. Near to this section of the line are sited Trimpley reservoirs and pumping station and aqueduct (see picture on page 20).

Northwood Halt, just under 2 miles from Bewdley, is a request stop for trains and not included in the timetable. About to pass through this beautifully restored halt on 18 September 1994 is 2–6–0 No. 46443 with the 2.05 p.m. Bridgnorth to Kidderminster train.

The next section of the SVR between Northwood Halt and the old Tenbury junction (or divergence) is about three-quarters of a mile in length. This area is very popular with photographers because of the open spaces near the trackside. On 29 September 1985 BR Standard Class 4 4–6–0 No. 75069 hurries through this section of the SVR with the 2.21 p.m. Bridgnorth to Kidderminster service. It is worthwhile making a comparison with the picture of No. 75069 awaiting restoration (page 48) and the above scene to see the high quality of the work carried out by the SVR at the Bridgnorth workshops.

Another beautifully restored engine, this time No. 3440 *City of Truro*, photographed near Northwood with the 11.20 a.m. Bridgnorth to Kidderminster train, also on 29 September 1985.

On 7 August 1994 No. 46443 drifts down past the site of Tenbury junction with the 2.50 p.m. dining car train from Bridgnorth to Kidderminster. Note the LMS buffet restaurant coach. The trackbed of the line to Tenbury Wells and Woofferton can be seen clearly in the foreground of the picture.

The 12 December 1981 was a brilliantly sunny winter's day, complete with a fairly heavy layer of snow. Also, happily, on that day the SVR were running their famous 'Santa Specials' from Bewdley to Father Christmas's grotto at Arley station. So it was a combination that was ideal for kids, rail buffs and photographers alike, who braved the elements on that beautiful but very cold day. Ex-LMS 2–6–0 No. 46521 looks a treat as it approaches Bewdley with a return 'Santa Special' from Arley on that icy December day.

A few minutes before the previous picture was taken GWR pannier tank No. 5764 is seen shunting empty coaching stock at the north of Bewdley station. Look at the icicles on the locomotive!

Over the years the SVR has had many
distinguished locomotive visitors including
Castle Class 4–6–0 No. 7029 *Clun Castle* from
Tyseley Railway Museum. No. 7029 is seen
leaving Bewdley with a train to Bridgnorth on
a wet 26 June 1982.

Although *Clun Castle* is a GWR design, it was actually built by British Railways (at Swindon) in 1950. It was withdrawn from BR service in December 1965, but was immediately preserved by Tyseley Railway Museum, and over the years has seen much work on the main line.

4

Bewdley to Kidderminster

On a very wintry 1 January 1979 ex-LMS Class 3F 0–6–0 tank No. 47383 heads over Wribbenhall viaduct and approaches Bewdley station with a return 'Mince Pie' special train from Arley. The use of a long lens also shows the caravan park (to the left of the smoke), which is situated on the other side of the River Severn. The Bewdley area is very popular with caravanners and holidaymakers as well as, of course, with fishermen.

A common sight at Bewdley – the token exchange – as GWR Manor Class 4–6–0 No. 7819 *Hinton Manor* pulls out of the station on 21 June 1981 with the 1.05 a.m. train to Bridgnorth.

Earlier I talked about the wintry conditions on 12 December 1981. Here are two more pictures taken on that photogenic day. Above is GWR 2–6–2 tank No. 5164 having just exchanged tokens, pulling away into Bewdley station with a return 'Santa Special' from Arley, to be greeted by (in the picture below) hundreds of eager children (and adults) all waiting for a trip to the grotto at Arley station. Snow, steam and Santa – what a magical combination!

On 31 March 1968 GWR 0–6–0 No. 3205 enters Bewdley station with a very important railway inspection train, from Bridgnorth to Bewdley and return. On board were a party of senior BR officers, including the chief surveyor of BR and the London Midland Region (LMR) surveyor. They were very impressed with what they saw, and pronounced the SVR competent to run a railway. And so the 'open weekend' of the following 13–14 April saw (members-only) trains run between Bridgnorth and Hampton Loade. (*John Dew*)

The enthusiasts' weekend of 21 to 23 September 2001 saw many locomotives at work on the line, including visiting engine ex-LMS Class 5 MT 2–6–0 No. 42765, seen here entering Bewdley on 21 September 2001 with the 11.55 a.m. service from Bridgnorth to Kidderminster. These sturdy-looking engines are popularly known as 'Crabs'. They were designed by George Hughes (formerly of the Lancashire & Yorkshire Railway and then of the LMS) and introduced in 1926 under the direction of Henry Fowler, who succeeded Hughes as chief mechanical engineer of the LMS.

Two more pictures taken on Friday 21 September 2001 at Bewdley station. This is GWR Class 9400 0–6–0 pannier tank No. 9466 shunting a beautifully restored 20 ton GWR 'Toad' brake van.

A few minutes after that picture was taken the 12.55 p.m. arrived from Bridgnorth, hauled by ex-SR West Country Class Pacific No. 34027 *Taw Valley*, at the rear of which was former Port Talbot Railway (later GWR) 0–6–0 saddle tank No. 813. This fine-looking engine was sold by the GWR to Backworth colliery in Northumberland in 1934, where it remained for thirty-three years until it was moved by road to the SVR, arriving at Bridgnorth on 25 November 1967.

A picture taken from the GWR footbridge at Bewdley on a damp 10 August 1974 shows GWR 0–6–0 pannier tank No. 5764 about to leave platform two with a Bridgnorth train.

A much brighter scene a few months earlier, on 26 May 1974, shows ex-WD 2–10–0 *Gordon* about to leave Bewdley with the 1.15 p.m. train to Bridgnorth, the service between Bridgnorth and Bewdley having commenced a few days before, on 18 May.

This view, taken on 1 August 1994, shows how congested Bewdley station used to get with empty coaching stock, etc. before the new carriage shed was erected at Kidderminster in April 2000. (See picture on page 108.) Entering the station is GWR 2–8–0 No. 2857 with the 1.30 p.m. from Bridgnorth.

This is the scene at Bewdley today, with SR West Country 4–6–2 No. 34027 *Taw Valley* entering platform three with the 12.55 p.m. Bridgnorth to Kidderminster train on 21 September 2001. In platform two is GWR pannier tank

No. 9466 on a goods train to Highley, and platform one is awaiting the next train from Kidderminster going forward to Bridgnorth. This is, possibly, preservation at its finest, and very reminiscent of the BR picture on page 23.

On a September day in 1972 ex-LMS Class 2 MT 2–6–0 pauses at Bewdley station with a works train from Bridgnorth. Note the headboard 'SVRS' – Severn Valley Railway Society – the original name of the association, formed in 1965 to save the line. The SVR Society in December 1969 merged with the SVR Company, which had of necessity been formed in 1967 to purchase the line. (*John Dew*)

Watched by a group of keen enthusiasts, young and old alike, GWR 0–6–0 pannier tank No. 5764 approaches Bewdley's number one platform with the empty stock for another 'Santa Special' to Arley on 12 December 1981.

Opposite: BR Britannia Class 7 Pacific No. 70000 *Britannia* stands in the yard at Bewdley on 1 April 1971. It was based at Redhill, Surrey, but moved to Tyseley on 15 March 1971 for wheel turning, and then on to Bewdley on 28 March and to Bridgnorth on 9 April. After seven years of restoration work by the Britannia Locomotive Society the locomotive was renamed by its designer Mr R.A. Riddles at a ceremony at Bridgnorth on 20 May 1978, and commenced running on the SVR the following September. A few years later, in the early 1980s, it moved to the Nene Valley Railway at Peterborough.

Bewdley station and the surrounding railway area has a fine array of GWR signals, as the next three pictures well illustrate. On the first day of 1979 ex-LMS Class 3F 0–6–0 tank No. 47383 shunts stock at the Kidderminster end of platform three, overlooked by a fine-looking bracket signal. Before the service started to Kidderminster in July 1984 locomotives arriving on trains at Bewdley would take water there, and be 'stabled' until the return working.

GWR 2–6–4 tank No. 5164 is seen next to a fine-looking GWR bracket signal as it waits for its return working to Bridgnorth, 1 January 1981.

To complete these three semaphore pictures, we see GWR Class 43XX 2–6–0 No. 7325 approaching Bewdley south signal box with an afternoon Kidderminster to Bridgnorth train. The train is framed by two beautiful sets of GWR signals, complete with wooden poles. 29 July 1994.

Although the service from Bridgnorth to Bewdley started in 1974, it would be another ten years, on 30 July 1984, before regular trains ran on the 3-mile section between Bewdley and Kidderminster. On this short section of the SVR the line runs through Bewdley tunnel (near Foley Park Halt, which closed in 1970) and then over Falling Sands viaduct, before reaching the SVR station at Kidderminster. Pictures of these locations can be found in the colour section. As the line nears the terminus it runs parallel with the Worcester to Birmingham line. On 7 May 1990, ex-LMS 0–6–0 tank No. 47383 approaches the end of the line with an afternoon train from Bridgnorth to Kidderminster.

Taken from the 'other side' on 26 August 1994, this picture shows 2–6–0 No. 46443 heading for the SVR station at Kidderminster with the 11 a.m. train from Bridgnorth. To the right of the train can be seen the yard and carriage sidings, etc. on which is built, as our next picture shows, a magnificent new carriage shed. This shed is a third of a mile long, with four tracks that can house up to fifty-six passenger coaches. It cost 2¼ million, 75 per cent from the Heritage Lottery Fund and 25 per cent from SVR shareholders, and was opened on 20 April 2000.

This view was taken on 13 October 2001, and shows Class 50 No. 50035 *Ark Royal*, 'Western' Class No. D 1015 *Western Champion* and, in the distance, Class 50 No. 50049 *Defiance*. A diesel maintenance depot is also planned to be built in this location. Also in this yard, but behind the photographer, is a locomotive turntable which came from Fort William. This was installed in 1994.

Turning round from the previous scenes, this is the view looking towards the SVR terminus. Here, ex-SR West Country 4–6–2 No. 34027 *Taw Valley* pulls away from the station with an afternoon train to Bridgnorth, 7 May 1990. On the right-hand side is the junction with the BR Birmingham to Worcester line. Also in this view is the former Kidderminster goods shed, situated behind the signal box and water tower, which was purchased by the SVR in 1985 and is used by the Company's carriage and wagon department.

This picture of 'celebrity' visiting locomotive LMS Coronation Pacific No. 6233 *Duchess of Sutherland* leaving Kidderminster with the 12.55 p.m. to Bridgnorth was taken on Saturday 22 September 2001, part of the enthusiasts' weekend. A comparison with the earlier picture shows new trackwork to the outer platform, and a run-round loop. On the loop line is ex-GWR 15XX 0–6–0 pannier tank No. 1501.

Also at Kidderminster station is the Kidderminster Railway Museum. This is housed in a former warehouse, just off the station concourse, and is visible on the extreme left-hand side of the two previous pictures. This is a most interesting place to visit, with many relics and artefacts from the past. There is also a café in the museum serving excellent tea, sandwiches and cakes, and a bookshop. From the museum café area it is also possible to see and photograph the trains. Visiting 'celebrity' locomotive No. 60103 *Flying Scotsman* – probably the most famous locomotive of all – waits to take out the 1 p.m. to Bridgnorth on 8 October 1994.

This is the fine-looking frontage of the SVR terminus at Kidderminster, which opened to the public in 1985. It incorporates a public house – The King & Castle – and at the rear are the gift/bookshop and station buffet. I should add here that both Bridgnorth and Bewdley stations also have buffet facilities, and Bridgnorth also has a well-stocked bookshop. The design of Kidderminster SVR station was based on a Great Western design from around 1900.

5

SVR Locomotives on the Main Line

Since the late 1970s many locomotives from the SVR have provided the motive power for special charter trains on British Railways. Here is a selection of the numerous workings undertaken by SVR engines over the years. 1985 was the year of the GWR 150 celebrations, with many special trains and events occurring throughout the year. The SVR supplied many of the locomotives for the trains and events, including arguably one of the finest preserved GWR locomotives, GWR Class 28XX 2–8–0 No. 2857. On 10 September 1985 No. 2857 ran from Kidderminster to Newport with a rake of mixed wagons and vans. While at Newport locomotive and train performed a special run-past from Alexandra Docks goods yard and, as seen here, through Hillfield tunnel and on through Newport station – a sight never to be forgotten, and also on a perfect late summer's day.

Also active in 1985 was another handsome GWR locomotive – Hall Class 4–6–0 No. 6960 *Raveningham Hall* – photographed here on 21 September 1985 as it climbs Cockett's bank west of Swansea with the 8.35 a.m. Swansea to Carmarthen special train. At the time No. 6960 was an SVR locomotive, but it is now based at Toddington on the Gloucestershire Warwickshire Railway. Note the headboard and the GWR coat-of-arms.

A rare visitor to the main line is ex-LMS Class 2 MT 2–6–0 No. 46521, seen here with another Valley stalwart BR Standard Class 4 MT 2–6–4 tank No. 80079 as they head up the Gloucester to Worcester line at Defford with a Didcot to Worcester special train. The date is 1 January 1995. Both these locomotives came to the SVR from Barry scrapyard in 1971, No. 80079 being owned by SVR members, and No. 46521 by SVR member Charles Newton. On the left-hand side of the picture can be seen the medieval bridge crossing the River Avon.

No. 43106 again, this time heading out of Chester across the Dee bridge with the southbound Welsh Marches express to Shrewsbury and Newport on 5 June 1982. The second locomotive is another SVR engine, GWR Manor Class 4–6–0 No. 7812 *Earlstoke Manor*. On the top right-hand side is the edge of Chester's famous race course. It can also be seen that this was originally a four-track section (as far as Saltney Junction, where the Shrewsbury and North Wales lines part company).

Opposite: On 11 October 1980 LMS Class 5 MT 4–6–0 No. 5000 and ex-LMS Class 4 MT 2–6–0 No. 43106 head north up Llanvihangel bank (near Abergavenny) with the 'Welsh Dragon' from Newport to Shrewsbury. No. 43106 has been on the SVR since 1968, but No. 5000 arrived in 1977 on loan from the National Railway Museum at York.

GWR Manor Class 4–6–0 No. 7802 *Bradley Manor* runs through the deep cutting just south of Wickwar tunnel (Gloucestershire) on the Birmingham to Bristol former Midland Railway main line with a Worcester to Newton Abbot charter train. 20 January 1996.

On 4 November 1995 GWR Class 43XX 2–6–0 No. 7325 hurries along the former GWR Paddington to South Wales main line at Coal Pit Heath with a Stourbridge Junction to Bristol to Swansea special train.

Two views of BR Standard Class 4 MT 4–6–0 No. 75069 at work. The picture above was taken on 21 August 1985, and shows No. 75069 crossing Frampton Mansell viaduct in the 'Golden Valley' just south of Stroud. The train is the 1350 from Gloucester to Swindon, one of the many run that year as part of the GWR 150 celebrations. In the picture on the right the 4–6–0 is seen on the old Southern main line from Waterloo to Exeter. The location is Milborne, just east of Sherborne, and the train is the 1500 from Exeter to Salisbury, 28 June 1992.

During the spring bank holiday week of 1987 a series of steam specials were run from Machynlleth to both Aberystwyth and Barmouth. One of the participating locomotives was GWR Manor Class 4–6–0 No. 7819 *Hinton Manor*, seen crossing Barmouth bridge on 24 May 1987 with an afternoon train for Barmouth.

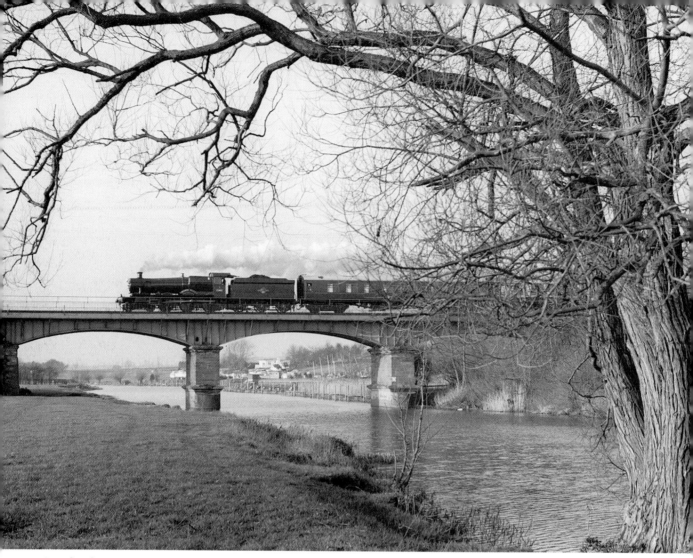

On a bright winter's morning, 20 January 1996, another of the Severn Valley's trio of GWR Manor Class 4–6–0s, this time No. 7802 *Bradley Manor*, crosses the River Avon at Eckington and heads south with a Worcester to Newton Abbot charter train. (See also picture on page 116.)

Opposite: These two pictures illustrate SVR locomotives on BR test trips. The picture above shows LMS Stanier Class 5 MT 2–6–0 No. 2968 and support coach running through Droitwich junction with a Kidderminster to Gloucester test run on 31 August 1996.

After overhaul at Bridgnorth Gresley Pacific No. 60009 *Union of South Africa* ran on a test trip from Derby to Sheffield and return on 22 February 1990. The return special was photographed on the four-track section at Tupton, north of Clay Cross junction, a scene not unreminiscent of the East Coast main line in the outer London suburbs, perhaps.

No. 3442 on the S&C climbing to Ais Gill summit on 24 March 1990 with a Carlisle to Blackburn train.

Opposite, top: During 1989 and 1990 LNER Class K4 2–6–0 *The Great Marquess* was active on the main line, including a stint on the Fort William to Mallaig line in the summer of 1989. On Saturday 8 July 1989 No. 3442 heads through Woofferton with a Hereford to Stockport charter train. This was the first stage of the journey to Fort William. On the following day *The Great Marquess* worked a special over the S&C from Leeds to Carlisle, all part of its northward journey.

Opposite, bottom: Once on the Mallaig line it was a regular performer, and is seen here at Loch Eilt on 24 July 1989 with a Fort William to Mallaig train. I should say here that, having made many trips to this line, this was the one visit when I was blessed with sunshine.

GWR Manor Class 4–6–0 No. 7819 *Hinton Manor* pauses at Tiverton Junction for a blow-up on a wet 7 April 1985. This train was from Bristol to Plymouth, and was the first steam passenger train to run on the main line in the West Country for over twenty years, also being part of the GWR 150 celebrations. Note also the lovely old GWR signal box, which would soon be gone with the Exeter re-signalling scheme.

Another 1985 GWR 150 picture, this time on 6 July at the summit of Llanvihangel bank near Abergavenny. GWR Hall Class 4–6–0 No. 4930 *Hagley Hall* and Castle Class 4–6–0 No. 7029 *Clun Castle* provide super power for a Kidderminster to Hereford to Cardiff special charter train.

Over the past decade an SVR locomotive that has worked on many special trains over a large part of the BR network is BR Standard Class 4 MT 2–6–4 tank No. 80079. Here, on 24 September 1995, No. 80079 is seen passing Langley sidings and approaching Langley station with the 1320 Snow Hill to Stourbridge Junction. A series of steam specials were run on that Sunday to commemorate the opening of the 'Jewellery Line' between Birmingham Snow Hill and Stourbridge Junction.

A long way from the previous picture, No. 80079 is at the rear of a Barnstaple to Exeter train at Cowley Bridge junction on 1 May 1994. At the front of the train is sister engine No. 80080 from the Midland Railway Centre at Butterley. These two locomotives have quite often worked together, either double-heading or – as in this case – 'top and tailing', there being no run-round facilities at Barnstaple.

The final picture shows SVR stalwart ex-LMS Class 5 MT 4–6–0 No. 45110 on main line duty on 7 November 1998, approaching Cannock station with a Birmingham to Walsall to Rugeley to Crewe train.

BIBLIOGRAPHY

Bannister, G.F., *Branch Line Byways, Vol. 1: The West Midlands* (Atlantic Transport Publishers)

Christiansen, Rex, *Forgotten Railways, Vol. 2: Severn Valley & Welsh Border* (David & Charles)

Geens, Barrie, *The Severn Valley Railway at Arley* (Wild Swan Publications Ltd)

Marshall, John, *The Severn Valley Railway* (David St John Thomas)

Williams, D.C., *Severn Valley Railway Visitor Guide* (Severn Valley Railway Company)

The 23 May 1970 was a very important date for the SVR, being the official re-opening day of the line. On that historic day GWR 0–6–0 No. 3205 is just about to leave Bridgnorth station at 2 p.m. with the 'Severn Valley Re-opening Train', bound for Hampton Loade.

The following day (24 May) ex-LMS Class 2 MT 2–6–0 No. 46443 is caught by the camera as it pulls out of Hampton Loade with a Bridgnorth train.

Winter and summer at Bewdley tunnel. Sporting an authentic Western Region reporting number, ex-GWR Class 4300 2–6–0 No. 9305 (now No. 7325) bursts out of Bewdley tunnel with a Kidderminster to Arley 'Santa Special' on 5 December 1992. (*Hugh Ballantyne*)

On 28 August 1994 Class 2 MT 2–6–0 No. 46521 leaves the tunnel with the 3.45 p.m. Kidderminster to Bridgnorth train. Note the lovely rake of GWR coaches.

Throughout the year on the SVR certain weekends are set aside for enthusiasts. Among these is a diesel weekend where the SVR diesels and visiting engines virtually take over the line and run a special timetable. On 20 May 1990 (during a diesel weekend) visiting locomotive Class 35 Beyer Peacock (Hymek) Type 3 diesel No. D 7076 was photographed in Bewdley cutting, just south of the station, with a mid-morning Bridgnorth to Kidderminster train. These hydraulic locomotives had a short life, being introduced in 1961, but being withdrawn by the mid-1970s.

After withdrawal in 1973 No. D 7076 spent six years at the BR experimental department at Old Dalby. It was privately purchased in 1979, and was restored at the East Lancs Railway at Bury, whence it returned to service in 1988. (*Malcolm Ranieri*)

To contrast with the above picture, we see a picture taken on a steam enthusiasts' day – 20 September 1986. Ex-LMS Class 3F 0–6–0 tank No. 47383 heads through Northwood with a southbound freight train specially run for the enthusiasts' weekend. (*Christina Siviter*)

The SVR 'Autumn Steam Gala' of 2001 was a three-day event from Friday 21 to Sunday 23 September. Among the visiting locomotives was Stanier LMS Coronation Pacific No. 6233 *Duchess of Sutherland*, newly restored to main line running.

On 21 September No. 6233 and a splendid rake of LMS coaches waits to leave Bewdley with the 1.05 p.m. Kidderminster to Bridgnorth service, while on the other track GWR 0–6–0 pannier tank No. 9466 approaches platform three with a freight train from Hampton Loade. (*Christina Siviter*)

On 18 March 1979 GWR Class 57XX 0–6–0 pannier tank No. 5764 runs by the side of Trimpley Reservoir with a Bridgnorth to Bewdley train. At the rear of the train is the waterworks. This location is roughly halfway between the Victoria Bridge and Northwood Halt.

Opposite: The early morning of 17 October 1993 (before the start of the working day) sees a fine line-up of locomotives at Bridgnorth shed and yard, including GWR 2–6–0 No. 7325, ex-LMS 2–8–0 No. 48773, GWR small prairie tank No. 4566 and GWR pannier tank No. 5775. (*Hugh Ballantyne*)

4–6–0 No. 7802 *Bradley Manor* crosses Falling Sands viaduct with a morning Kidderminster to Bridgnorth train on 22 December 1996. This seven-arch viaduct, which crosses the River Stour and the Staffordshire & Worcestershire Canal, is situated on the outskirts of Kidderminster about a mile from the SVR terminus. (*Malcolm Ranieri*)

BR Standard Class 4 MT 2–6–4 tank No. 80079 pauses at Highley station on 23 August 1980 with a Bridgnorth to Bewdley train. Note the beautifully restored station/stationmaster's house and the GWR signal box, behind which can be seen a GWR 'mechanical horse', built for local deliveries of heavy parcels, etc. I was privileged to be given a 'look-round' the inside of the stationmaster's house by the then stationmaster (and former musical colleague and friend of mine) Barrie Geens, and I would say that it is just as immaculate inside as outside. The gateway on the extreme right leads to the River Severn. (*Christina Siviter*)

Winter sunshine highlights GWR 2–6–2 tank No. 4566 at Bewdley on 1 January 1979. In the background by Bewdley South signal box is 0–6–0 saddle tank No. 193.

Among the special events held in 2000 was a heavy horse and vintage transport weekend. On 11 June 2000 a fine-looking pair of shire horses are seen in the yard at Highley station in company with a vintage Shand-Mason fire engine, which was built in 1901 and is named 'Florian'. Manning this splendid machine, once of the Birmingham Fire Brigade, are firemen from the West Midlands Fire Service. This fire engine is now owned by the West Midlands Fire Service, and it can often be seen at rallies and other events.

On the same day outside Kidderminster station was a display of vintage motor vehicles, including this late 1950s BMC BRS parcels wagon, once a familiar sight on our roads. (*Both: Malcolm Ranieri*)

Probably the most photographed location on the Severn Valley Railway is the Victoria Bridge, which crosses the Severn just south of Arley. It was erected in 1861 and designed by John Fowler. The picture above shows a close-up of the bridge, with GWR 0–6–0 No. 3205 heading over it with a Bridgnorth to Bewdley train on 20 June 1982.

The long view of the bridge below was taken a few years earlier on 10 April 1977, and shows ex-LMS Class 2 MT 2–6–0 No. 46443 with a Bewdley to Bridgnorth train. This locomotive is still in the red livery in which it had been painted for the film *The Seven Per Cent Solution* (filmed the previous year on the SVR).

The attractive Oldbury Viaduct, just south of Bridgnorth, is the setting as visiting engine GWR Castle Class 4–6–0 No. 5029 *Nunney Castle* crosses its five arches with the 3.45 p.m. Bridgnorth to Kidderminster service on 8 May 1994. (*Hugh Ballantyne*)

LNER Class A3 Pacific No. 4472 *Flying Scotsman* and a rake of LNER teak coaches make a fine sight as they climb out of Bridgnorth on the morning of 22 September 1991 with a train bound for Kidderminster. (*Malcolm Ranieri*)

A stormy sky and winter sunshine make for ideal lighting conditions as GWR Class 51XX 2–6–0 tank No. 5164 races through Northwood with a Hampton Loade to Bewdley train on 1 January 1981.

On 24 April 1988 2–8–0 No. 2857 nears Bewdley tunnel with an empty coaching stock train from Bewdley to Kidderminster to form the 11.55 a.m. Kidderminster to Bridgnorth service. In the background is the southern boundary of the West Midlands Safari Park. (*Hugh Ballantyne*)

One of the SVR's fine fleet of diesel locomotives, former BR Sulzer Class 25 No. D 7633 (formerly No. 25283) pulls out of Kidderminster station on 26 August 1994 with a breakdown train, including a 6 ton capacity steam crane. This crane was built by Smiths of Rodley, Leeds, in 1949 for the Western Region of BR, and spent most of its 'life' at Radyr, Cardiff.

To complete this trio of Kidderminster pictures is Manor Class 4–6–0 No. 7802 *Bradley Manor* pulling out of the SVR terminus with the 1 p.m. to Bridgnorth. The date of this picture is the start of the new millennium – 1 January 2000.

Opposite: This telephoto shot of Kidderminster station, taken on 28 April 2001 (part of the Diesel Gala weekend), shows well the station buildings, etc. and also, on the left-hand side, Kidderminster Railway Museum. In the station itself is Warship (hydraulic) Class diesel No. D 821 *Greyhound*, complete with 'Bristolian' headboard, waiting to leave with a morning train to Bridgnorth, while on the right-hand side is light engine No. D 1013 *Western Ranger*, one of the three Western Class hydraulic diesels on the SVR. (*Hugh Ballantyne*)

We finish this selection of colour views with two pictures of SVR locomotives on the main line. On 26 May 1987 GWR Manor Class 4–6–0 No. 7819 *Hinton Manor* and a rake of GWR coaches enter Dovey Junction with the 0940 from Machynlleth to Barmouth.

It is not just the SVR steam fleet that is in demand for main line charter trains; so too are the Class 50s diesel locomotives. No. 50031 *Hood* is seen climbing out of Liskeard (near Bolitho) with a return Penzance to Paddington charter train on 18 July 1998.